Livin' Beyond Your Paycheck

Moving From **Not Enough**
Into **More Than Enough**
While Making The Same Pay!

By Winfred Chad McKendrick

The Grace of God, Inc.
Orlando   Los Angeles

Scripture taken from *The Message*. Copyright © 1993, 1994, 1995, 1996, 2000, 2001, 2002. Used by permission of NavPress Publishing Group.

Scripture taken from the New King James Version. Copyright © 1982 by Thomas Nelson, Inc. Used by permission. All rights reserved.

Livin' Beyond Your Paycheck by Winfred Chad McKendrick
457 Pickfair Terrace
Lake Mary, Fl 32746

Published by The Grace of God, Inc.
Marina Del Rey, CA 90292
www.graceofgodinc.com

Copyright © 2007 by The Grace of God, Inc.

Cover design by Oddball Dsgn. Photography by Angelo Davis.

ISBN: 978-0-9800947-0-1

Published 2007. Printed in the United States of America.

www.livinbeyondyourpaycheck.com

Warning – Disclaimer

This book is intended to provide information and guidance on the topic of budgeting and personal financial management. It should in no way take the place of applied common sense and or sound advice from a qualified Financial Counselor who has intimate knowledge of the specifics of your financial situation.

Every effort has been made to make this book as accurate and complete as possible. However, there may be mistakes, both typographical and in content. Therefore this text should be used only as a general guide and not as the ultimate source for your financial well-being. Furthermore, this book contains information on the finance industry that is current only up to the printing date.

The purpose of this book is to educate and entertain. The author and The Grace of God, Inc. shall have neither liability nor responsibility to any person or entity with respect to any loss, damage caused, or alleged to have been caused, directly or indirectly, by the information contained in this book.

Contents

Dedication

I would like to dedicate this book to my wife, Tammy, for all of the support a man could ever ask for. Thank you for following me as I followed Christ.

To my children, Chad II & Amanda, I thank God for Chad praying for our house and Amanda for being the princess of the house.

To my friend, Patrick Wright, who stuck by me and advised me in the hard places of my life.

Acknowledgements

I would like to recognize and thank the following individuals who made this project possible:

My parents, Winfred & Betty McKendrick, David & Ollie Betton, and Frank & Nora Woodard; My Sisters, Shelly McKendrick, Amii McKendrick, and Tawana Allen; My Nieces & Nephews, Tiana Davis, C.J. Davis, Paige Davis, Tyre' Allen, and Leonard Allen, Jr.; My Grandparents, Rev. Silas (Phyllis) McKendrick, Joe (Rosa) Paige, Frances Betton, Rev. Curtis (EvaLou) Rivers, Robert (Amanda) Clayton, and Julius (Katie) Gordon and in memory of my favorite aunt, Lena Pearl Devine, who always believed in me!

I thank God for an extremely supportive FAMILY!

FOREWORD

You don't have to walk far to run into somebody who is having financial problems. As a pastor, advisor and counselor to many, I see the issue of finances penetrating every part of the human experience. But it goes much deeper than that. And it's about time somebody showed us that this is also a spiritual issue!

Minister Winfred Chad Mckendrick is the man for the job! He has taken this tough subject and broken down solutions in a way that anyone from the average Joe to the CEO can receive it and walk away empowered to do something different to change their situation. In *Livin' Beyond Your Paycheck*, he reveals powerful exercises in faith and discipline that can be applied to get you out of debt and free yourself to do the things that God put you on Earth to do!

I have seen this strategy work in my congregation and in the lives of many who've had the honor of sitting in a room with Chad for more than a few minutes. It's infectious! And that's exactly how the truth ought to be!

Do not delay one more minute in your quest to move *from not enough* and into *more than enough* today!

In Him,

Rev. Willie C. Barnes
Macedonia Missionary Baptist Church, Eatonville Fl.

INTRODUCTION

One hundred and thirty-one point three percent.

One hundred and thirty-one point three percent.

Come on: Say it out loud with me.

One hundred and thirty-one point three percent.

Go ahead. Feel free to ask me.

"Why are we chanting 'one hundred and thirty-one point three percent' together?"

Because you are probably one of the Americans who can identify with it. You probably can say that there is way too much month left at the end of your paycheck. You probably can say that you are barely making ends meet. And you are probably sick and tired of it. I know I was.

131.3% is the average American household debt compared to disposable income. What does that mean? It means that the average American owes $131.30 for every $100 that they have to spend. It means you may be in serious trouble. But it also means that you are not alone.

Every single day in every single city in our country, somebody goes to bed wondering how they are going to make ends meet because their paycheck just isn't enough. They are stuck in a rut and don't know how to get out. They work hard for their money, but still never seem to have quite enough to get ahead. They are living paycheck to paycheck and they are just one missed payday away from eviction, hunger and despair. They need to make radical changes in the way they have been doing things. They need this book.

And since, you've read this far, I bet you do too.

The subject of budgeting or finances is scary. I understand why. For many of us, money is one of those things that affects all areas of our lives, yet there always seems to be a limited amount to go around. It seems like just when we get our minds wrapped around our finances, something unexpected happens that throws everything out of balance again. It's scary because we've done so many wrong things in our pursuit to get it right.

Believe me, I've been there and done that. Throughout this book, I'll share with you some of the worst money mistakes I've made and (*more importantly*) some of the best decisions I've made to help me come out of the money rut that so many of us find ourselves in. I found that it all came down to learning and unlearning habits. You can trace your poor money habits all the way back to what you did with your allowance as a child, or how you spent your earnings from your very first job. You probably made poor choices even then. But it's not all your fault. I'm willing to bet that no one ever taught you the basics of money management.

Let's start there. Who taught you about how money works? It's a simple question, but most of us don't have an answer. We can remember who taught us to work hard for money so we could pay our bills. That was our family. We can remember who taught us that racking up high balances on credit cards was not a good idea. That was collections agencies. We can even remember who taught us to be giving, no matter how little we had. That was our church or spiritual advisor. However, we can't remember anyone sitting us down to actually explain how money works or how we could get it to work *for* us. That's the story for me, at least. No one ever taught me that there was more to responsibly handling my money than just paying all of my bills on time. If there is a Money 101 course, I never took it and I haven't met anyone else who's taken it. And, since you're still reading this book, I suspect you haven't either.

That's where I come in. I want to help you see money in a way that you probably have never considered. I want to show you how – no matter how much (*or how little*) money you make – your money can begin to work for you!

But first, we've got to undo some serious damage. If you are anything like the average American, that 131.3% is your reality. You have spent time, energy, and maybe even money trying to figure out how to "stretch" your paycheck further, but nothing worked. The problem is, you may have been asking the wrong people. You may have been turning to someone for guidance who didn't know any more than you. You may have been seeking advice from someone whose financial situation was no healthier than yours. If you want to learn how money works, shouldn't you go to someone who is successful with their money?

Take me, for example. About fifteen years ago I was a successful, college-educated, highly motivated young man who worked as a financial counselor. You'd think I was a credible resource, right? Not quite. No one had ever taught me what to do with the money that I earned, so I was in just as bad – if not worse – shape than the folks who were coming to me for guidance. On paper, I looked like a great resource for financial advice. I had money in my retirement accounts. But I had no money in the bank. I was living paycheck to paycheck, and I wasn't even doing a great job at that! Yet, I gave advice every single day to people who were determined to live beyond their paychecks. It took me a while to realize that the problem was not just in the clients' poor spending habits, but also in my poor advice. I was giving them the same advice I had always been given.

"Direct a certain amount of your paycheck into a retirement account."

"Pay your bills as soon as you get paid to avoid being late and accruing fees."

"Keep your credit score high because credit is more valuable than cash."

"Blah blah blah...."

That was poor advice because it is exactly what *doesn't* work for anyone whose paycheck is being stretched as far as it can be and is still not making ends meet.

The good news is through a friend, research, study and experience; I learned some powerful lessons that I have applied in my own life to turn my finances around. And now it's your turn. Consider yourself warned, though. The techniques I suggest in this book are "out of the box". This is not your typical approach to budgeting. And it should not be. Typical budgeting systems don't work for people who are one paycheck away from eviction or financial ruin. Drastic times call for drastic measures. Are your finances in a drastic state? Hang on: I have just the plan for you!

Before you go any further, answer these questions:

1) Am I one of the millions of Americans who is living just barely within my paycheck?

2) Am I willing to make drastic changes to fix my

finances?

3) Am I ready to do something different to better my life and the lives of my loved ones?

4) Do I know someone who could use the tools in this book to better their life?

If you answered YES to two or more of those questions, read on. If you did not, I suggest you keep reading anyway. I guarantee you will find some nuggets of wisdom to help you make better financial choices.

This is the part where most people break into a cold sweat. If you feel your heart starting to palpitate, relax. This is a simple plan that will make a HUGE difference in your life. I have taught this strategy to students as low as the second grade. If seven year olds can learn the concept, I'm sure you can too.

This story changed my life! Take a look at the next few pages and see if you can find yourself in it.

The Story About Investment

It's also like a man going off on an extended trip. He called his servants together and delegated responsibilities. To one he gave five thousand dollars, to another two thousand, to a third one thousand, depending on their abilities. Then he left. Right off, the first servant went to work and doubled his master's investment. The second did the same. But the man with the single thousand dug a hole and carefully buried his master's money.

After a long absence, the master of those three servants came back and settled up with them. The one given five thousand dollars showed him how he had doubled his investment. His master commended him: 'Good work! You did your job well. From now on be my partner.'

The servant with the two thousand showed how he also had doubled his master's investment. His master commended him: 'Good work! You did your job well. From now on be my partner.'

The servant given one thousand said, 'Master, I know you have high standards and hate careless ways, that you demand the best and make no allowances for error. I was afraid I might disappoint you, so I found a good hiding place and secured your money. Here it is, safe and sound down to the last cent.'

The master was furious. 'That's a terrible way to live! It's criminal to live cautiously like that! If you knew I was after the best, why did you do less than the least? The least you could have done would have been to invest the sum with the bankers, where at least I would have gotten a little interest.

'Take the thousand and give it to the one who risked the most. And cast the unprofitable servant into the outer darkness.'

Matthew 25:14-30 The Message and NKJV

Did you find yourself in there somewhere? What would you have done with the money? No matter what you might have done, you are about to learn what *to do*. The right way to manage your money is just a few pages away. So take a few breaths, find a comfortable chair, a pad and a pencil and get ready to change your life!

*Everyone thinks of changing the world, but no one thinks of changing himself . ~**Leo Tolstoy***

1

UNDOING THE DAMAGE

Changing The Way You Were Taught To Think About
The Money You Earn

What's the first thing that pops into your mind when you think about the money that you earn? Is it your car note or your phone bill or your mortgage payment? Is your mind flooded with thoughts of due dates and late fees? If so, you've got it all wrong! Your money issues are mind over matter. If you can train yourself to think differently about your money, you can get your money to behave differently for you. It all begins in your mind.

Do you need to pay your bills? Yes you do. In fact, you don't just need to pay your bills. You need to be *responsi-*

ble in paying your bills. But bills should not be the first thought in your mind when you think about getting paid. If it is, then you are neglecting some key principles of money management. You are forgetting that in order to truly receive, you must first give. Your first thought about money should be *sharing*. But, I'm getting ahead of myself here.

For now, let's work on the way you see money. Do you see money as a limited resource that must be hoarded for a rainy day? Do you think of money as only a means to live and eat? Do you work to live or live to work?

Let's do a simple exercise to find the answers. Pull out your wallet or purse or wherever you keep your cash. How is it arranged? Are dollar bills stuffed into a side pocket? Are they crumpled and facing many different directions? Is your change purse full of lint, old mints and gum wrappers? Is there loose change all over your house and car? If so, we've got to tackle the topic of *respecting your money*. Believe it or not, money deserves respect. They say *"money makes the world go 'round"*, right? What about *"money is the root of all evil"*? The scripture actually says that the LOVE of money is the root of all evil. But the point is the same. Money is very powerful. Those who value, respect and protect it are often those who have an abundance of it.

Go ahead. Ask me the questions that just popped into your head. *"What do you mean, Chad?" "Are you saying that I should treat money as if it was a person?"* No. Not exactly. What I am saying is that if you treat money like it is a powerful tool that many wars have been fought over and many history-changing events have been decided over, you will better understand the impact it can have on your world way beyond paying your bills.

Think about how important money is to many areas of your life. You need money to eat and provide shelter. Which means you need money to *survive*. You need money for transportation, which means you need money to get to work to pay for transportation. You work for money, yet you need money to work. Money is cyclical – which means it goes in circles. And the work/transportation cycle is not the only cycle that money moves in.

A bank is a place that will lend you money if you can prove that you don't need it. ~**Bob Hope**

When I counsel people about their finances, I also hear frustration about the credit/debt cycle. Think about it. You need good credit to get a loan. But you won't need a loan if you have good credit because you are probably in a pretty stable financial place. So, how does the person who needs the money the most get it without being able to prove they are responsible enough to manage a loan? The sad truth is often they don't. The loan is not offered to that person, and they remain stuck in the credit/debt cycle fending for themselves. There's that word again – cycle. The problem is, the cycle has been taking money in the direction *away* from you. I want to help you change the direction of your money cycle. Let's reverse the money cycle to get it to flow back into your pocket.

When we were small children we learned to care for things that are important to us. My kids value their favorite toys more than gold! Whether it's my son with his favorite video game or my daughter and her favorite doll, each child goes to extra trouble to make sure the precious toys are in their rightful place when they are done playing with them. They pay special attention to keep them clean and in good working condition. They don't allow their friends to play rough with them. My children treat their favorite toys with the same care and respect that we should use when caring for money. I'm not saying that you should "wash and fold" your dollar bills. That would be obsessive. I am saying that you should take care of your money. Keep dollars orderly and facing the same direction in your wallet or billfold. Organize change in one place. Keep checkbooks and deposit slips in one location that is organized for easy access. Treat money as a valuable resource that is the key to reversing the negative financial cycle in your life.

Are you still not convinced? I've heard of couples fighting until they were on the brink of divorce over twenty dollars! In fact, money is one of the top reasons why couples divorce in our country. Are you wondering how something so trivial could ruin a marriage? Have you ever lost money because you were being hasty or careless? How did it feel when you realized it was gone? Awful, right? It's a much different feeling than losing something that has little or no value. After all, money is powerful. That's the underlying factor in divorces that are caused by financial reasons. Couples argue and fight over where money was spent, how they are going to pay for priorities, what are priorities, etc. Arguments about money become the center of the marriage, infiltrating discussions about everything. Couples find that they cannot discuss where to go for vacation, what to eat for dinner, or who to invite to the kids' birthday party without money becoming a major factor in the conversation. This drives many couples to become distant, and ultimately, to divorce. And we haven't even gotten into the couples that lie to each other about their spending habits! Are you starting to see why money deserves respect? Good!

Now, how do we respect money? *The key in treating money with respect is in acknowledging that it has power, and behaving accordingly.* Honor the fact that it has the ability to find itself back to you if you care for it and spend wisely. You will learn that it can even multiply before it gets back to you. If you change your habits, you can change your life. Treating your money with respect is one habit that, if applied daily, can and will change your life. Let's learn how.

Exercise: Devise a one-woman or one-man search party around your car, house, office, etc. in search of neglected and forgotten money! Check under car seats, couch cushions, in old handbags and wallets, in sock drawers, etc. You'd be surprised where dollars and cents may be lurking. Collect all of your findings in one location. Count it and then separate it with purpose! Align all dollar bills facing the same direction in your wallet, in order of increasing value. Dump all litter out of your change purse or wallet and place only <u>clean</u> coins in that area. If necessary, wash dirty coins before putting them away. This is the first step to respecting your money! The rest is easy. Just take the time and make the effort to organize your money any time you add or remove any from your wallet. You will quickly begin to see what a major difference this will make in the way you see your "chump change", and eventually the "big bucks" you will have once you apply this program.

The easiest way for your children to learn about money is for you not to have any.

Katharine Whitehorn

2

Child's Play

One Little Boy + Three Cans = Lifelong Wealth

Remember the question *"who taught you about how money works"* that I asked in the Introduction? When my children are asked that question, they will have an answer. They will say that their parents taught them a solid system for the money that they earn. I hope your children say the same about you. This program is not just for you, but also for the many generations who will come after you who will rely on this knowledge to live comfortably and still have enough to share with the world around them. I teach this program to my children because I cannot afford not to. I share my knowledge with them to help them become wise and responsible enough to know what to do with their own wealth one day.

My son Chaddy has got it down pat! No matter how much money he makes on allowance, he separates it into three cans – his *Save* can, his *Spend* can, and his *Share* can. If he gets $1.00, he takes $.25 and puts it into his Share can, puts $.25 into his Save can, and $.50 into his Spend can. That's the 25-25-50 plan! It's the children's version of what you will learn to apply in your finances.

On Sunday mornings, Chaddy is excited to get up for church! He sees church as his opportunity to share with others. He springs out of bed, gets dressed with purpose, and grabs his "Share" can. He empties the contents of the can into his palm and gingerly places the money into this pocket. All the way to church he is smiling, his hand covering the pocket where his precious stash is stowed. You can just see the anticipation on his face as he waits anxiously through service for the time when the minister calls for the congregation to give an offering. Some Sundays, he places the whole pocketful onto the offering plate. Other Sundays, there is less because he has shared some with his little sister, Amanda, who may have come to church empty handed. No matter what, Chaddy is eager to Share because he knows that his small gift, combined with the gifts of others, will go a long way toward helping our church and our community at large.

Chaddy's "Save" can doesn't get emptied nearly as frequently as his Share can. In fact, it has never been emptied. Right now, the purpose of Chaddy's Save can is to teach him the concept of saving toward a big, long-term goal.

The Save can is for college. It's not for his tuition. His mother and I are saving for our children's tuition in our Priority Savings (more on that in Chapter 5). But Chaddy's Save can is for *his* priorities in college. Once he gets to high school, my wife and I will begin to talk with Chaddy about deciding on a priority list to use the Save can toward. We'll guide him through making responsible choices with the money. Ultimately, it is his to spend, because he is the one who would have been so responsible in saving it for all those years.

Because he'll be a teenage boy, we can assume he will have priorities like a new car, or maybe fixing up the "starter" car we might have bought him for high school. Those are definitely priorities for a college student. Some other items might include traveling abroad during school breaks, or buying a four-bedroom townhouse to rent out three rooms to friends after the thrill of dorm rooms has worn off. He may even decide to *not* spend it and instead continue saving for a post-college dream like his first home. Whatever Chaddy decides to spend his Save can on, the concept of responsible saving is being rooted into his mind even now and will stick with him for the rest of his life.

The Spend can is Chaddy's to spend whenever and however he wants. This is his yummy candy, new toy, *"ooh daddy can I have that?"* can! I tell him *"spend it fast, spend it slow, spend it all, there ain't no more!"* Sometimes the contents of the Spend can last until the next allowance payout. Sometimes they don't. But practicing this plan has made Chaddy much more responsible in his spending. He has learned to avoid impulse shopping by making choices about what he really, really wants today, versus what can wait until later. That will be key in him becoming a responsible spender as an adult.

Teaching my kids to separate their money into cans encourages a very important and responsible behavior. It deters them from spending it all as soon as they get it and encourages them to focus on the purpose of the money first. That's what you need to do.

Designating Funds

Imagine you work at a convenience store. After a couple of hours of working, can you decide how much money you should have made and then just remove that amount of money from the cash register and put it into your pocket? No! Of course not! What do you do instead? You allow your employer to take their money first, then separate it out how they see fit. Employers understand that a percentage of the money must go to pay for the lights, some to maintenance staff, some to supplies, and so forth. A percentage of every dollar that comes in is already designated to various parts of the business even before it is made. That's what I want you to begin to do with your paycheck.

Let's go back to the cans. My son has three cans that he separates by 25%, 25% and 50% for Sharing, Saving and Spending. That's the simple, childlike way of budgeting. For adults, I encourage you to split your paycheck into *four buckets*. Yours should be broken down this way – 10%, 10%, 20% and 60%.

The first 10% is Sharing. Sharing includes Tithing to your church, charitable gifts to organizations, and gifts to others who are in need. This will be further explained in Chapter 3.

The Second 10% is your Stash (which is a form of Savings). The Stash is your extreme emergency savings account. It is cash stored someplace in your home. This will be further explained in Chapter 4.

The 20% is your Priority Savings. Priority Savings is the account where you place the money that is being saved toward big, long-term goals. This is your typical Savings account – but with new rules! This will be further explained in Chapter 5.

And the 60% is your Operations (or Spending) bucket. This is the place where bills are paid, groceries and gas are purchased, and everyday expenses are covered. This is the one that frightens people the most. Don't you dare close this book! You can and will learn to live on 60% of your income, and have some to spare! The subject of Operations is further explained in Chapter 6.

If you begin to automatically separate every dollar you make this way, it will become harder to get sidetracked and splurge or spend all of your paycheck as soon as you get it. One of the first things you will need to do is to break your paycheck into weekly parts. That's easy if you get paid weekly. But if you are paid every two weeks or once a month, you will need to divide out your money into 1-week increments and then apply the budget I've outlined. Over time, you will become used to breaking down your budget into this system and only using each bucket for its designated purpose. It will become second nature.

I deal with mutual funds, life insurance and mortgages. The way I came to this system was through meeting with tons of clients who wanted my services but they were in such a bad place financially, they could not participate in any of the services I provided. This is the plan that has changed my life and many of my clients' lives. All you need is a Savings account, a Checking account, a Stash place in your home and a determination to stick it out. You can do this, right? We are going to look at each bucket separately so that you get a good understanding of how this process can and will work for you. Let's get going!

Exercise: Do the math now. If you get paid weekly, bi-weekly, or monthly, divide your pay amount into increments of 10%, 10%, 20% and 60% to see how much money you are expected to distribute to each bucket. Now you know exactly how much you have to work with in the following chapters.

Next, write out all of your expenses. Think about everything - *I mean everything* - that you spend money on each month. Hold onto that list as we begin to describe what goes into each bucket so that you can categorize each expense.

Do not be discouraged! You can do this. Just take it one week at a time, and you will be well on your way to life-long wealth!

If a man is proud of his wealth,

he should not be praised until it is known how he employs it.
~Socrates

3

GIVING BACK

What Rich People Know That Could Change Your Life

We've learned that there are three major activities tied to your money. They are Sharing, Spending and Saving. Most people know all about spending and saving, but don't really consider sharing as a constant in their financial program. In this chapter, you will see why I don't just consider sharing to be important. I consider it to be *the most important* action you can take with your money. In fact, Sharing is the very first bucket that I want you to focus on with every dollar that you earn and with every paycheck that you receive.

Think about someone who you know that is relatively well

off. Is that person giving? Would you consider them to be generous? Be careful here. Whether or not this person has ever given *you* anything should not play into your answer. Do they give *in general*? Is there a cause or church or need that they are passionate about that they regularly contribute to? 9 times out of 10, your answer will be yes. Have you ever heard the term *"the rich get richer and the poor get poorer"*? I am convinced that that statement is true based upon the habits that many rich people apply in their daily lives. I believe that wealthy people have figured out the value of giving in relation to remaining wealthy. Not convinced? Hang in there, I'll show you what I mean.

The list of the richest people in our country includes lots of big names that you are familiar with. Let's start at the very top with the person who was known as the richest man world for over ten years - Bill Gates. You may know of Bill Gates as the chairman of Microsoft who is worth somewhere over $50 Billion. What you may not know is that he is credited with having donated nearly $29 Billion to charitable causes since the year 2000 and continues to give through his Foundation. Bill joined with his wife, Melinda, to form the Bill and Melinda Gates Foundation – an organization that provides funds for college scholarships for under-represented minorities, AIDS prevention, relief for diseases prevalent in third world countries, and other causes.

What about Warren Buffet? He's known as the second richest man in our country. He amassed his wealth through investments. In 2006, Warren Buffet announced that he would donate $30 Billion to the Bill and Melinda Gates Foundation.

The rich giving back is not a new concept. Have you ever heard of John D. Rockefeller? Bill and Melinda Gates sure have! Get this: There would be no $30 Billion contribution from Warren Buffet to the Bill and Melinda Gates Foundation if there were no foundation, right? Well, there would not have been a foundation if Bill and Melinda Gates were not influenced and guided by their friend David Rockefeller – the only living grandson of the oil tycoon John D. Rockefeller! It is common knowledge that Bill and Melinda Gates sought the expertise of David Rockefeller in how to be charitable based on his grandfather's reputation for being such a generous giver during his life.

So, John D. Rockefeller - who is recognized as *the richest person in U. S. history,* by the way - was a giver? You got it! And, his giving has set off a chain reaction that is touching billionaires that are alive and well today? Yep! Do you want to know how you can get in on all of this giving? I'll be happy to tell you.

Let's not forget Oprah Winfrey, though. Do you remember the Oprah episode when she gave away all those cars to people who needed transportation? That was the first time anything like that had ever been done on national television. Oprah Winfrey has literally changed the way the world looks at giving back by developing philanthropic organizations such as her Angel Network and schools for girls in developing countries. And she continues to develop new ways to give back each year!

Many people say that people like Oprah Winfrey and Bill Gates and Warren Buffet have too much money. While I don't think that is possible, I get what they are saying. Those three people do have more money than they can think of ways to spend it. That's why they form founda-tions that distribute money to a number of different causes. And, as long as they continue to give, money continues to find its way back to them so that they can plant it into the world again. That is exactly how you can get in on all the giving! Give of what you have, and see what happens next!

I remember a saying that I heard once as a child in church. Someone said, *"you just can't out give God!"* I thought it was funny at the time, but I've come to fully understand the meaning. Whether you believe in a God or a Creator or the Universe, the principle is the same. You reap what you sow. The more you give, the more it comes back to you… often times way more than you gave out.

Spending vs. Sharing

Spending and Sharing might seem to be similar, but there's one major difference. Spending represents you. The very act of spending implies that you give money in order to *acquire* something in return. On the other hand, Sharing represents others. Sharing means giving money or time or resources, expecting absolutely nothing in return. And that's exactly how you should apply it in your life. Sharing should not be practiced with the expectation of receiving. Give because it is *the right thing to do*, with no ulterior motives. Give willingly because you have it and so many others do not. Give and it will come back to you.

Methods of Sharing

For me and my family, sharing means tithing. We give 10% of our income to our local church in accordance with our beliefs. It is something we do cheerfully (*remember little*

Chaddy in church?). It makes us feel like our money has purpose when we can apply it to fulfill a law of our faith and also help our community. We trust our church to use the money from our tithe to distribute to the areas of our community where it is needed most.

For some families, sharing means giving a regular donation to a charitable organization or to causes that they are passionate about. When giving to organizations, do your homework to become comfortable with where your dollars will be spent. Ask to see financial reports and research the charity's track record in the community or in supporting their cause. There are a number of websites that make it simple to research charities. Many charities are also on file with the Better Business Bureau. That's a great place to begin fact-finding to ensure that your money goes exactly where you intend for it to.

To other families, sharing is simply being a resource for people in their lives who are in need. I want to caution you on this one. We all know someone in our family who spends irresponsibly and always finds themselves in a bind. Be careful not to take that person's hardships on as your own. You may need to establish some hard and fast rules to avoid becoming a crutch for people who do not spend wisely. My rule is to never do anything for anyone that they can and should do for themselves. If something unexpected happens once and puts your friend or relative in a bind, they *should* be able to turn to you. But, if something unexpected happens *every* month, consider that your friend or relative may be making unwise decisions to put themselves into bad positions because they know they can depend on you to bail them out. You should let them read this book!

If saying NO is a real issue for you, there might be some underlying insecurities at play. Are you seeking approval or acceptance? Do you thrive on being needed by others? These are deep-seated issues that will need to be checked before you can be successful in any budgeting program. Remember, you cannot save money if you do not have money! You cannot have money by making unwise investments – which include investing in friendships or approval through gifts. If the people in your life require money to love, appreciate or approve of you, you may need to re-evaluate the people in your life!

Whatever "Sharing" means to you and yours, it is a time-honored principle that attracts great things back to you. As you manage money better, more flows to you. You must think beyond your job as a source of income. You must rise above living paycheck to paycheck. This is the way to begin. If you want to be like the wealthy, you must begin to think like the wealthy NOW. Don't wait until you have extra to spare. That will never happen at the rate you are going. But it will happen if you change your habits - starting today!

SHARING: PAYCHECK PRINCIPLES

#1 Never compromise the 10% that is designated to sharing.

#2 Give because it is the right thing to do, not because you want something in return.

#3 Share with an organization or person that you trust to use your funds wisely.

#4 Don't do anything for anyone that they can do for themselves. That only enables irresponsible behavior and cripples them from becoming independent.

Exercise: Since you completed the Chapter 2 Exercise, you know exactly how much money goes into your share bucket. Given that, will you donate the entire bucket in one place? Or will you spread it out over a few organizations/causes/people? Make a list of all the areas that you would like to contribute to. List anything and everything that interests you. You may decide to give to a different place every month. That is perfectly fine. You should do whatever makes you feel the best about giving back a small portion of what you have earned to help someone else who is in need.

Reviewing that list, take each name listed and begin to research whether or not this is a sound cause, organization or person to donate time and money to. If you have an existing relationship with the person or group, that may be an easy answer. If not, I encourage you to do your homework. Quick researches on the Internet are often all you will need to do to know enough about whether or not the organization is legitimate and will make good use of your funds.

When you are done, narrow down the list to whatever number you are comfortable with. Then, decide how often and how much of your Sharing bucket you will contribute to each area. Now you have a solid plan for Sharing! Great Job!

Let's move on to start Saving!

The more you chase money,
the harder it is to catch it.

~Mike Tatum

4

Stashing Cash

The Extreme Emergency fund

Savings is the second priority after Sharing. While the meaning of Sharing and Saving is different, the purposes are similar. Both are intended to have an impact on your future. *Sharing* creates habits that turn the money cycle back into your direction. *Saving* creates habits that hold onto money for use at a later time.

We are going to discuss two different types of Savings. Most of us are familiar with the second type that will be covered in the next chapter. In fact, you probably have a separate Savings account that you put aside a certain percentage of each paycheck into. That is not the Savings that I want to talk about right now. Now, I want to talk about your *Stash*.

Your Stash is a CASH pile stored somewhere in your home. I suggest placing it into a secure place that only you and your spouse have access to. Why would you need a Stash? Because you need money in a secure place in your home that you can get your hands onto in a crunch.

I'm probably dating myself here, but do you remember playing cops and robbers as a kid? If you were the robber, what were you after? The Stash, right? Let's think of your Stash in this way. Think of it as your own personal goldmine – your hidden treasure. It's a very precious and valuable reserve in your home that NOBODY knows about. I mean *nobody* but you and your spouse. Lock it in a safe, store it in a storage bag in the freezer, or maybe even hide it in a little box under a floorboard. Do whatever you have to do to make sure that it is not easily accessible by anyone – even you. You do not want yourself or anyone else to be tempted to remove money from the Stash.

Many people turn to their regular Savings accounts so often that they are depleted when the need for something urgent arises. Your Stash is your *extreme emergency fund*. It's not just a rainy day fund, but a *hurricane, tornado, earthquake, flood, tsunami day fund!* It is the place that you can turn to when there are no other options and you need cash fast. Hear me on this one: The stash is not for paying bills except in cases of extreme emergency – like an impending eviction, natural disaster, or illness.

The Stash Can Be A Life Saver

My wife and I were so thankful a few years ago when our Stash came in handy. It was during the summer that Central Florida was hit by back-to-back-to-back hurricanes. There was mass panic because banks were closed and some people lost access to their money when ATMs ran out of cash. But we had our Stash on hand and that got us all the way to my in-law's house in Georgia to wait the storms out comfortably. That's the whole purpose of the Stash. It's the pot you will pull from when funds are tight and you find out that you have to book a flight someplace to be with a sick relative. It's the pile of cash that you can turn to when you need to get out of a major bind without disrupting the other parts of your finances.

One of my clients told me recently about how her stash came in handy. As she and her husband were driving across the country from Florida to California, something malfunctioned on their car. They found themselves stranded somewhere in *Middle of Nowhere, Texas*. At first, they panicked, thinking of all the unplanned costs this could mean. They would have to pay for a tow truck, then possibly stay at a hotel a few nights, then ultimately pay to get the car fixed so they could complete their journey. Their credit cards had high balances and they were already traveling on a tight budget. Any extra expenses could mean trouble – big trouble. But then they remembered the Stash. Just as they were leaving home for the journey, they had grabbed the stash and tucked it away in the glove compartment of the car – *just in case*. To their relief, the Stash came in handy at the perfect time! It was enough money to cover the tow, hotel stay and car repairs! They actually ended up enjoying that little detour on their journey, and learned about a part of our country they would never have even heard of otherwise! The Stash saved the day!

Another client shared her Stash story with me. She had experienced a devastating family tragedy that resulted in a legal battle. If you know anything about our court system, you know that trial dates are hardly ever concrete. She was going to be called as a witness in a trial that was over 2000 miles away, but she would have no more than a couple of days' notice when the trial date was finally set. Reluctant to purchase a flight in advance and then have to pay more fees to cancel it, she waited patiently to be told that the trial would proceed. Finally, after over a year of waiting, she was called on a Thursday afternoon and told to be present for trial on Monday morning. Instead of running up credit cards, she used her Stash to pay cash for the airline ticket! Thanks to her Stash, she made it to court in time to testify and didn't have to disrupt her finances because of it!

Stories like this continue to pour in as people rely on their stashes to get out of tight binds. Notice I did not say that they went into the Stash for a new pair of shoes or to throw a party. In all three cases, the Stash remained untouched until it was desperately needed. And when that time came, it was a lifesaver.

Building Discipline With Your Stash

Building discipline with your Stash will not be an easy thing to do. I remember being tempted to empty the Stash every single month when we first began this program. After all, it was a wad of cash just *sitting* there, right? No! It's not there at all. Consider it as spent money as soon as you lock it away. Do not give it another thought until you absolutely need it.

DETERMINING A CAP

Another thing to consider regarding your Stash is setting a limit that you will not let it grow beyond. I won't advise you to keep tens of thousands of dollars on hand in your Stash as you are still working towards finding room in the rest of your budget. That would not be wise. Decide what your limit will be. For most people it's a round number like $1000. Once your stash hits whatever your limit is, move the overage to your Priority Savings account. It can be used there to save towards long-term goals, and to help you alleviate stress in your monthly budget.

REMOVING MONEY FROM THE STASH

Another point to be clear on is what to do after removing money from your Stash. You cannot borrow money from your Stash. Once you take it out (either for an extreme emergency or to transfer to your Priority Savings), you do not need to consider replenishing it. When the money is gone, it's gone. To replenish it, simply stay on the program. Each week, continue to Stash away 10% of your earnings, and it will grow again in time. There is no need to stress about paying yourself back. You have simply used the money for its purpose, and the time has come to begin again with your savings goals.

The Stash is one of the controversial parts of this system. People seem to be reluctant to store cash in their homes for a number of reasons. If safety is a concern for you, think long and hard about a place where you know that no one would consider looking. One couple told me that their Stash is stored in an airtight bag placed in the back of their toilet! Can you imagine? I'll take their word for it! The point is, you want to feel safe at home. You don't want to feel as if you are taunting someone to break in and find your stash. To answer that concern, simply do not tell anyone about the Stash in the first place. Use common sense. If you let people know that each payday you bring home 10% of your pay and hide it somewhere in your home, that may cause them to become curious. For that same reason, not even your children should be aware of your Stash.

Good old-fashioned discipline and common sense are required for this part of the program to work. It is going to take some real effort on your part to ignore the temptation to spend and to not mention your Stash to anyone. Trust me, you can do it. The only way to know is to try, right? Nothing beats a failure but a try!

<u>Stash: Paycheck Principles</u>

#1 Go to your Stash as a last resort. Never ever touch the Stash unless it is an extreme emergency. Set up a scenario in your mind that would constitute an extreme emergency. That way, when those "everyday" emergencies come up (and you know they will), you will have already established a certain criteria to compare it against. If it is not on the same level as your "made up" scenario, DO NOT GO INTO YOUR STASH!

#2 Set a limit for your Stash. For some it's $500. For others it's $1,000. Choose a challenging but realistic goal for yourself. Once you hit that limit, move the overage amount into your Priority Savings account (see chapter 5).

#3 If you have to pull money out of your Stash, do not feel pressured to pay it back. You cannot loan money from the Stash. It is there for use in an emergency. To replenish it, you only need to stick to the plan and soon it will be back to a sizable amount.

Exercise: Start now by writing a list of all the possible Stash places in your home. Test yourself by hiding something insignificant in those places… maybe paper cut up into fake dollar bills. How often do you pass by your Stash location? Is it a place you will encounter everyday? Will that temptation drive you to "raid" your Stash? If so, choose another location. Do this until you have found a place that is comfortable and discreet. Some people live in crowded places with no privacy at all. They choose to store their Stash in a relative's home or with a friend that they can trust. If all else fails, purchase a safe that requires a combination or key to open. Then, hide the key or combination in another place in a different part of your home.

You have what it takes to make this program work. But *it won't work until you work it*. So, what are you waiting for?

If you would be wealthy,
think of saving as well as getting.
~Benjamin Franklin

5

PAYING IT FORWARD

Priority Savings

Have you seen the movie *"Pay it Forward"*? If you haven't, rent it today. The moral of the story is good because it encourages everyone to do random acts of kindness to complete strangers to set off a chain reaction of goodness in the world.

I love the concept of that movie because it sums up what I believe Sharing and Saving do you for. Get this! When you share and save, you are moving forward. You are taking actions that move you into a better future. When you pay your bills you are standing still. You are only placing a bandage on a "today" scratch that will appear again in 30 days! If I am only paying bills all the time, where am I going? Nowhere! And I am sure you would agree that *nowhere* is the last place you want to go with your finances! I am ready to go somewhere financially, aren't you?

That brings us to the rest of your Savings. 20% goes to PRIORITY Savings. This is not about saving for a rainy day. It's about saving for future <u>needs</u> such as retirement, buying a new car, house, new appliances etc.

First Things First

Before you can even begin to think about savings for new things, you must set your self up to be safe in the event of an unforeseen job or income loss. Therefore, the very first goal of your Priority Savings account should be to save up <u>6 months</u> worth of living expenses. Yes, you read that right. Do the math. Figure out exactly how much it costs you to live every month. Multiply that amount by 6. That should be your first Priority Savings goal.

So many of us are living paycheck to paycheck and literally run the risk of becoming homeless if we miss just one payday. This program was created to help you live beyond paycheck to paycheck and get out of that rut! Once you reach your goal of 6 months of Savings, then you can start working toward saving for things like retirement, a new car, etc.

Setting Priorities

Decide for you and your family what your priorities are and stick to that list. If you are nearing retirement age, you may want to save aggressively towards a secure future. If your car is on its last leg, it may take priority. If rent/mort-gage is a huge part of your budget, allow yourself to pull from Priority Savings *when necessary* to ensure that rent never goes unpaid. Whatever you deem as your set list of priorities, establish the list and try not to deviate from it on a monthly basis.

The Priority Savings account is similar to the Stash in that you only go into that account for needs. Most people who attend my seminars have Savings accounts that they con-tribute to every pay period, but also draw from just as fre-quently. I have a little dance for this called the "put-take" (*it's similar to the hokey-pokey and looks just as silly*). You put the money in, then you take it right back out! Who is that benefiting? How will you ever save that way? The only way you can save money is by *not* spending it!

Priority savings is your opportunity to *Pay it Forward* into your own future. It's your chance to plant seeds today that will continue to grow so that you can reap a huge harvest when the time is right. It's your security blanket when the job market seems unstable or illness sneaks up on you. It's your parachute to make sure that you land safely when life shakes you up.

A New Lesson From An Old Parable

Do your remember The Story About Investment in the beginning of the book? It's an age-old parable filled with age-old wisdom. In the story, the master goes away on a journey. But, before he leaves, he entrusts three of his ser-vants with money. The first two servants saw that as an opportunity to increase their master's wealth. They invest-ed the money wisely and watched it grow. The last servant

– who was full of fear and doubt – didn't do anything with the money. When the master returned, he had the exact same amount that he had been given originally. The master became outraged when he found that the servant did not do anything with the money. He did not invest it or grow it in any way. In fact, all he did was bury it in a hole. That would have been fine if the master had given the money to the servants to hold onto "just in case", or as a Stash. But this was a test. The master wanted to see what creativity and ingenuity the men would apply to grow the seeds that he had planted in them. He wanted to see how they would "pay it forward".

The resourcefulness of the first two men impressed the master. He saw them as men who he could trust with even more responsibility because they had been faithful and wise over the little amounts while he was away.

The last servant, however, was an altogether different type of man. He was operating in fear and doubt and he allowed that to consume him. He was afraid to invest the money with the bank, out of fear that he might lose it and anger his master. Fear can paralyze you into making unwise choices. The key to making this program work in your life is overcoming that fear, because scaredy cats never make money! (More on that in chapter 8)

EARNING INTEREST SHOULD INTEREST YOU

Your Priority Savings account should be a high-yield savings account with your bank. That means that it should be making interest – as much interest as possible. This money should be working for you. It should be constantly growing. That's the reason why the Extreme Emergency Fund is moved over to the Priority Savings account once it hits a certain limit. You don't want to have huge piles of money just sitting in your home. That money should be *growing!*

Determining a Cap

You should also determine a cap for your Priority Savings account. The truth is, savings account interest rates will only yield a couple of percentage points. You want your money to grow at double-digit interest rates! A good cap may be the amount of 6 months of living expenses that you calculated earlier. Once the money in your Priority Savings account hits that amount, move it to a mutual fund. A mutual fund is a company organized for the purpose of making investments. A mutual fund gets its capital from private individual investors, who allow the mutual fund to decide where to invest their money. You can learn more about mutual funds from your bank or a financial counselor. They are an excellent avenue to invest your money in order to see it grow at double-digit rates.

Removing Money from Your Priority Savings

Lastly, we must also cover the topic of removing money from your Priority Savings account for reasons other than re-investing it into a mutual fund. Like we discussed regarding the Stash, you cannot borrow money from your Priority Savings. Once you take money out (for a need on your Priority List), you do not need to consider replenishing it. When the money is gone, it's gone. To replenish it, simply stay on the program. Each week, continue to Save

20% of your earnings, and it will grow again in time. There is no need to stress about paying yourself back. You have simply used the money for its purpose, and the time has come to begin again with your savings goals.

This is your path to wealth. Not every one will be brave enough to attempt this. If you want to change, you will. Everyone can start here because we are talking *percentages* – not set amounts. Everyone can break their paycheck down into 4 buckets and designate those buckets for specific purposes. Everyone can save toward things that are priorities in their lives. Everyone can live beyond paycheck to paycheck – even you.

<u>Priority Savings:</u>

<u>Paycheck Principles</u>

#1 Open a Priority Savings account with your bank that has a high interest rate.

#2 Set aside 20% of every paycheck as Priority savings until you have saved 6 months of income.

#3 Make a set Priority List that you are saving towards and do not change it.

#4 Only go into the Priority Savings account for Priorities.

#5 Once your Priority Savings account reaches a certain amount (set a cap for yourself), move the excess money into a mutual fund account with a high yield. The purpose of this is to have a certain amount of "untouchable" savings that continues to grow for you towards your goals.

#6 If you have to pull money out of your Priority Savings Account, do not feel pressured to pay it back. You cannot loan money from Savings. It is there for you to use on priorities. To replenish it, you only need to stick to the plan and soon it will be back to a sizable amount.

Exercise: Write out a list of your Priorities. Take into account everything that you want to start saving toward. This could include your children's education, a new home, a new car, a wedding, retirement, etc. If you have concern that your Operations budget may not cover your necessities like rent/mortgage or car payment, you may list those on your priority list as well. The list should be specific to what you and your family consider being most important at this time.

When you have identified all of your priorities, the list may be rather long. You may need to prioritize your priorities! Which of these is most important? Can the new car wait? If so, move it further down the list. But don't remove it. You want to feel free to use your Priority savings on a new car if the need one day becomes more urgent. Reorganize the list often, assessing what it is you value as savings goals.

When you are done, you will have a strict list of the ONLY items that you will allow yourself to dig into Priority Savings for. This way, you will not even be tempted to do the *"put-take"* dance and pull money from your Priority savings account unless it is for the pre-set list of priorities for you and your family.

Hang in there: You are well on the way to financial freedom. Doesn't it feel good?

Now is no time to think of what you do not have.
Think of what you can do with what there is.
-Ernest Hemingway

6

You Expect Me To Live On How Much?

Operations

Here comes the part that scares people the most. Hang on! I have not brought you this far to lead you astray! You can and will make this plan work for you if you set your mind to it!

Let's quickly review what we have learned. We know that money is powerful in our society and deserves respect. We know that we must designate every dollar that comes into our home into different buckets with specific purposes. We know that only paying bills is not the way to move forward and live beyond paycheck to paycheck. We know that we can practice the "pay it forward" principle by sharing money with others and saving for emergencies and priorities.

Now, it's time to discuss the part that applies to everyday life – the 60%. After you have Shared and Saved, you must handle your Operations. Operations means bill paying and daily living expenses. Operations are paid from the money that is left in your checking account after you have distributed the rest to Share and Save. It's the money in Chaddy's *Spend* can.

I know, I know. Most people say that they can hardly live on 100% of their money. 60% sounds impossible. Believe me, it's not. What if you were to make some adjustments? Cut back on some things? Cut out some things that are not priorities? Put off some things until later? You'd be surprised how far your dollars could stretch.

I Need Cash Now!

(But At What Price?)

I recognize that we are a quick-fix society. That's why so many "Get Cash Now" or "Cash For Your Car" signs blink along the highway. I've been to those payday advance places and found myself in another horrible cycle. At one point in my life, the cashiers knew me by name. They knew that I would do something to put myself in a position to need a payday loan every month between paychecks. I got to that place by making bad decisions and by allowing myself to become pressured into making non-priorities into priorities. You have to know that these places thrive on your fear and impatience!

For example, I allowed harassing bill collectors to bully me into spending my paycheck on old debt instead of paying for my priorities like rent and power. When the power bill went unpaid, I was threatened with service disconnection and quickly ran to get a quick loan to pay to keep the lights on. This ugly cycle only drove me deeper and deeper into debt and added to the list of people who I owed. Fear does not fit into the process of living beyond paycheck to paycheck! We'll talk more about fear in the next chapter.

Let's get back to the subject of paying our bills out of the 60%. Operations is the toughest part of the process for people to master because it requires discipline – even more discipline than not touching the Stash. Operations is the place where every bill is paid. So, in order to use your 60% effectively, you've got to know how to pay bills. Of course you know how to write checks and drop them in the mail. That's not what I'm talking about. I'm referring to the method *behind* paying bills. There is a right and a wrong way to go about it. The problem for most of us is nobody ever taught us the right way.

There are three new habits you need to consider when paying bills.

#1 Pay your bills weekly.

#2 Pay bills according to priority.

#3 Pay bills on the date that they are due.

Let's look at these habits one at a time.

Pay Your Bills Weekly

Since you have already done the math, you know exactly how much money you have weekly in your Operations bucket. You should also have gone down your list of expenses identifying which were Donations and which where Savings Priorities. So, everything left on your list must either be Operations or things that do not need to be in your budget at all. Looking pass the non-necessities, let's begin to organize your Operations bills. This may take some work. Find as many account statements as you can. For bills that you pay online, pull up the accounts on your computer. Take note of the due dates. If they are due during the 1st thru the 6th of the month, put those bills in a pile labeled Week 1 Bills. Do the same for Week 2 Bills (7th – 14th), Week 3 Bills (15th – 21st) and Week 4 Bills (22nd – 31st). Congratulations, you have organized all of your bills by the date when they are due! That is a huge step toward organizing your operations budget!

Since you already know how much money exists in the Operations bucket weekly, a few quick calculations should tell you if you will have enough to cover your bills each week. Do not panic if you find that you will come up short some weeks. That's where #2 comes in.

Pay Bills According To Priority

Most people find themselves coming up short during the first several weeks of bill paying on this program. To help you get around this little bump in the road, you will need to make some tough choices ahead of time. Prioritize your bills from ones that *must* be paid each week, down to bills that technically *could* wait. That will require work on your part. You may need to contact some of your creditors to ask if they can move due dates. You may have to pay some of the low priority bills late a time or two until your finances correct themselves and you begin to work out of a surplus instead of a shortage.

Pay Your Bills On The Date That They Are Due

Paying your bills too far ahead can set you up for failure by the end of the pay period. Many of us get paid on the first, then immediately pay all of our bills – including those that are due at the end of the month. But what if you need that money for something more important than one of those bills before the end of the month? You will have prioritized a bill over a real priority.

For example, let's say you have a balance due on an old department store credit card. It's due on the 27th of every month. Let's also say you get paid once a month on the 1st. Do you mail a payment to this credit card company on the 1st? No way! There is way too much month left and you have no idea what else may occur that is more important than that credit card payment. For the sake of this example, we'll say that some minor emergency arises like an unforeseen expense on the 20th. Perhaps one of your kids requires an extra piece of sports equipment for their big game. Do you pull the money out of Priority Savings? No way! That's not on your priority list! Do you pull it from the Stash? Nope! That's only for extreme emergencies! Do you pull it out of your Share bucket? Never! The only option you have is to pull this money out of Operations. But you won't be able to do that if your Operations account is empty from paying bills!

In reality, you could have waited to pay the credit card bill with the money that was left in your account during Week 4.

What If There's Not Enough Money?

It's possible that there would not have been enough in your Operations bucket to pay for that old credit card after you took care of greater priorities. If not, you could have contacted the credit card agency to let them know that you would not be able to pay this month, or to arrange to pay a lesser amount. In the worst-case scenario, you might have gotten penalized for missing a payment. Isn't the penalty worth being able to provide for your children and, in the end, set your family up to be more financially stable? You will have to take a few hits in this program. You cannot be afraid of consequences, or you have lost even before you begin.

Floating Priorities

Some of the expenses listed might have included everyday essentials like gas and groceries. You know those are Operations costs, but you may be having trouble guessing exactly how much to budget for them because the amounts fluctuate weekly. Those are called *floating priorities*. They are items that are constant in your budget, but you may never pay the same amount for them. You may drive more during some weeks than others, requiring more or less gas. You may eat differently from week to week, making it hard to put one number in your budget for food.

Consider this: *You don't have to fill up the car or fill up the fridge as frequently as you do.* For budgeting sake, begin by just getting enough to make it from week to week. Your goal is to come to a constant number for your budget. If you spend $50-$75 a week in groceries, budget $75 to be safe. Be flexible as far as how much you allow yourself to spend in these areas. Once you know how much they will generally cost, you can factor them into your budget as constant amounts with high priority.

What If I'm Still Coming Up Short?

If you find yourself still coming up too short to pay for priorities, then you can reach into your Priority Savings. Make sure that the items you are paying from Priority Savings are items that you have already listed as Priorities so that you will not deviate from the plan. If your Priority Savings is not enough to carry you through, depend on your Stash for extreme needs. Those needs might include a pending eviction or car repossession. Those are urgent and important needs that you can justify paying out of your Stash. If you keep up the plan you will not need to dig into your Stash or even your Priority Savings soon. You will learn to be completely operational out of the 60%. Don't believe me? Try it and see for yourself!

Operations: Paycheck Principles

#1 Assess your bills weekly, paying them according to priority.

#2 Communicate with creditors to plan your month effectively.

#3 Let go of fear.

#4 Consider Floating Priorities as bills that may fluctuate weekly and budget them accordingly.

Exercise: Now that you have learned how to apply each of the four buckets to your finances, you should be ready to practice the system. Jot down any questions or fears that you may have about moving forward. If there is an area that is unclear, take this time to review the previous chapters. Look for answers to the questions that you have listed. Review your expenses. Did you designate all of them to a bucket? What's left? Is it a necessary expense? Remember, you are trying to save money and grow your finances. There is no room in this plan for a beginner to be frivolous with their spending. Make purposeful choices about your money starting from this point forward. Make a decision to apply all that you have learned to ensure a better tomorrow for you and your loved ones. Your financial future depends upon you really *getting* the lessons in this book. Are you ready?

The only thing left now is to DO IT! Let's go!

Knowing is not enough; we must apply!
Johann Wolfgang von Goethe

7

PLUG AND PAY

Exercise

The time has come to plug your own budget into the system to begin walking your path to lifelong wealth! Are your palms getting sweaty again? Fear not! This plan can and will work for you. Remember: *It cannot work until you work it.* Application is the key!

One of the tools that I find most useful in this program is the *Livin' Beyond Your Paycheck Worksheet*. This form will help you lay out your entire budget. It will allow you to see all the numbers in black and white in one place. It is essential in organizing your money as it flows in and out of your hands. At the end of this chapter, you will find a blank

Livin' Beyond Your Paycheck Worksheet for reference. Take your time. Study it. Copy it down onto a tablet for your own use. This will become a handy reference as you begin to apply this program weekly.

Looking over the blank sheet, you can see that the top reminds you of the four buckets and the purposes of each. 10% is to Share with others. 10% goes into your Stash (*last result, extreme emergency cash on hand*). 20% should be deposited into your Priority Savings account. And 60% should be deposited into your checking account for Operations (*bills, food, gas, etc.*).

To help you become familiar with filling in the worksheet, we'll walk through a sample exercise. We'll call this person John. John makes pretty good money, yet he never seems to have enough to cover his expenses. He used to think that all he needed was a raise and everything would be ok. Since reading this book, John knows he could get a handle on his finances if only he could get organized. Sound familiar? Good! Let's begin.

John has walked through the entire process in the book. Beginning in Chapter 1, he has completed every exercise. He organized his spare change, wrote out all of his expenses, figured how much his weekly budget was for each bucket, decided on a Stash location, and set his priorities. You can find John's lists at the end of this chapter. John's *Livin' Beyond Your Paycheck Worksheet* is also at the end of this chapter for your reference. Fill in the sample sheet with your own figures as we walk through John's budget. This will help you become more comfortable working with the form.

As you can see, John's take-home pay every week is

$1000. The first thing John needs to do is to fill in his weekly income on each of the four lines (*a., b., c., d.*) provided. You should have already done the math to figure out what your take-home pay is weekly, so you can fill in those lines on the blank sheet, as well.

Next, separate your income into the buckets by percentages. In a $1000 paycheck, Share = $100 (1,000 x .10), Stash = $100 (1,000 x .10), Save = $200 (1,000 x .20), and Operations = $600 (1,000 x .60). You can fill in the spaces for Share, Stash and Save for all four weeks because they should not fluctuate (*e., f., g., h.*).

Week 2, 3, and 4 Operations should remain blank. Week 1 is the only week that Operations is certain. Why? Because after Week 1, you will likely have left over money each week that will need to be carried over (added) to the Operations line of the next week. Don't worry. It will make sense as we move along. For now, just write in your Operations amount for Week 1 and leave the other weeks blank. John will begin with $600 in week one (*i.*).

Now that we have listed all of the income that we can, let's turn our attention to the lower part of the *Livin' Beyond Your Paycheck Worksheet* - where bills are listed. Under Week 1, there should really only be rent/mortgage. No other bills should be due during the first week of the month (see the next chapter for more info on this).

John's rent is $1000 a month. Uh oh. John doesn't have enough money leftover after Sharing and Saving to pay his rent. This week he only has $600. Where can John pull the rest from? Well, Savings is considered a Priority Account. Is rent a priority? Yes. So, John *could* pull it from there. It is not yet an extreme emergency so John can't touch the

Stash yet. <u>If eviction is not imminent John shouldn't pull it from anywhere else yet – including Priority Savings</u>. The goal is to save money. John should wait until next week when his finances replenish. Since the first thing John did was to share, surely money is on its way back into his hands. Hang in there and have faith! You cannot afford to fear at this point.

If John pushes rent/mortgage into week two, all of a sudden there is another $600 (k.) in Operations available and he can now afford to pay rent. This is key for those of us who just do not have enough money to pay our bills. Juggling is necessary at first. *You must juggle to make a profit.*

In our example, John moved all of his bills from Week 2 to Week 3 after paying rent (m.). This freed up a good amount in the last two weeks of the month for bill paying. He listed his other bill amounts in the weeks that they were due (*p. through t.* and *w. through y.*). Then, he evaluated weekly which bills were priorities according to the amount he had available to spend.

<u>Move some things to the following week if they are not important enough.</u> Repeat this each week until Week 4. If you end up short, you may need to make some phone calls. Ask a creditor if they will accept less for this month if you need to. If they are priority bills, go into your Priority Account. If they are emergencies, go into the Stash. But whatever you do, do not fear!

If things work out for you the way they did for John, you will be in *surplus* at the end of the month. Imagine that! As you can see from the example, John ended up with $600 dollars to take into the beginning of next month. He has enough to pay rent during the first week of next month! He also has $400 in his Stash and $800 towards his Savings Priorities. He has already prospered from just one month of the program.

You May Not See A Surplus Right Away

For the first five months on this program, my wife and I were dipping into our Savings and Stash every month. Soon, we realized that we didn't have to do that anymore. After a while, we were going into Priority Savings only. Then we began to manage our money well enough to never go outside of our Operations money.

You can do this. Be careful not to get frustrated. The first time will be the most difficult as you try to find your way through the muck that is your finances. Once you have it, you will be so happy that you invested the time and effort!

Happy Budgeting!

Exercise: Continue to practice filling in *Livin' Beyond Your Paycheck Worksheets*. Begin to work the system. Read the next two chapters for encouragement along the way. Pat yourself on the back!

John's Priorities:
Rent
Retirement
New Car
Wedding

John's Expenses:
Rent - $1,000   *operations*
Groceries - $100   *operations*
Insurance - $150   *operations*
Phone - $50   *operations*
Water - $20   *operations*
Car - $400   *operations*
Gas - $80   *operations*
401K - $400   *savings*
New Car Down payment - $400   *savings*

LIVIN' BEYOND YOUR PAYCHECK WORKSHEET

10% _____

10% _____

20% _____

60% _____

	Week 1	Week 2	Week 3	Week 4
Income	$____	$____	$____	$____
Share	$____	$____	$____	$____
Stash	$____	$____	$____	$____
Save	$____	$____	$____	$____
Ops	$____	$____	$____	$____
Bills				
	$____	$____	$____	$____
	$____	$____	$____	$____
	$____	$____	$____	$____
	$____	$____	$____	$____
Sub total	$____	$____	$____	$____
Balance $	$____	$____	$____	$____

John's Livin' Beyond Your Paycheck Worksheet

10% - Share with others

10% - Stash

20% - Priority Savings (See priority list)

60% - Operations (bills, food, gas, etc.)

	Week 1	Week 2	Week 3	Week 4
Income	a. $1000	b. $1000	c. $1000	d. $1000
Share	e.$100	f. $100	g.$100	h.$100
Stash	e.$100	f. $100	g.$100	h.$100
Savings	e.$200	f. $200	g.$200	h.$200
Ops	i.$600	l.$1200	o.$800	v.$1080
		($600 + $600)	($600 + $200)	($600 + $480)

Bills

	j. $1000	m. $1000	p.$100	w.$400
			q. $150	x.$80
			r.$50	
			s.$20	
Subtotal			t.$320	y.$480
Balance	k. $600	n.$200	u.$480	z.$600

The greatest mistake you can make in life is to be continually fearing you will make one.

~Elbert Hubbard

8

SCAREDY CATS WILL NEVER MAKE MONEY!

Moving Beyond Fear And Into Faith

Many people will review this system. Many will want to start right away. But many will allow fear to deter them from making the best decision they could ever make for their finances. Will you be one of them? Will you be a *Scaredy Cat*?

Let's go back to *The Story About Investment*. One of the things that strikes me most about this story is the third servant's fear. That servant resembles a lot of people whose finances are in a never-ending cycle *away from* them. They are too blinded by fear to see their options. Think about it.

Fear is a huge factor in the way so many of us live our lives. We become so blinded by a fear of trying that we cannot see opportunity staring us right in the face.

Consider the homeless person standing in front of a fast-food restaurant holding a sign that says *"will work for food"*. The average person may think, *"They're standing directly in front of a place that may be willing to hire them. If they're willing to work for food, why won't they go inside and just apply?"* That's just the point! Now, barring any major psychological condition that may make them a danger in the workplace, there really is no clear reason why this person wouldn't just approach the owner or manager and offer to do something for pay. Even if sweeping the parking lot is the only responsibility that the restaurant can offer, isn't that *working for food*?

Much like the servant in the parable, the homeless person may be blinded to opportunity by fear. Not only can fear blind you, it can also paralyze you. Think about someone who is stuck in his or her ways. Somewhere along the way, they might have become afraid of change, afraid of challenge, or afraid of growth. No matter what the fear is of, it has caused them to stop moving, to stop progressing. They say anything that is alive grows and anything that grows changes. What if you stop changing? Do you stop growing? Do you stop living? Yes. And fear is at the root of it all.

Courage is not the absence of fear, but the strength to do what is right in the face of it. ~*J. Johnson*

I'm not saying that you should not be afraid. What I *am* saying is that you cannot let fear control you. You must move forward along the path to lifelong wealth in spite of your fear! You cannot keep doing what you have always done and expect new or different results. You must make changes – *no matter if you are afraid of change or not* – to see new results in your life.

If there is anything that I've learned about fear, it's that it breeds where there is lack of knowledge. In order to overcome your fear, you will need to first figure out what it is you are afraid of. Once we identify what scares you the most, we'll apply some knowledge to help you overcome it.

Remember our discussion about being dependent upon doing things or giving gifts to people to make them like or approve of you? That is rooted in a fear of not being accepted or loved. You may need to do some deep soul-searching to find exactly what is holding you back from pursuing a better future for yourself. Meanwhile, we'll talk about three common fears that deter people from applying this process in their lives. They are:

#1 Fear of losing your home

#2 Fear of credit and creditors

#3 Fear of family and friends

Let's tackle them one by one.

Fear Of Losing Your Home

I can understand anyone's concern over having (*or not having*) a place to lay their head at night. For me, that was the scariest part of not being financially stable. I had a wife and two small children. I was supposed to be the protector and the provider. *What kind of man puts his family in jeopardy of losing their home? How could I ever forgive myself if we lost our home?* I have learned that while those are valid concerns, they were rooted in invalid fears.

The biggest contributors that fed into my fear were mortgage company creditors. For you, it may be a landlord. These are the people who your rent/mortgage payment is due to every month. But they are also the ones who show no mercy when you are just one day late. They threaten to toss your belongings onto the street, to sell your home from right under you, to ruin your credit forever. The important thing to remember is that <u>you have rights as a renter and as an owner</u>. No one can take your home away if you are a few days late. And, according to this plan, you should never pay more than one week late. For homeowners, the foreclosure process takes months. You have time to make up a missed payment and get back into good standing with your mortgage company. Do not fear.

I am not encouraging you to be careless about your rent or mortgage payment. This is a very serious topic and I want you to take it seriously. What I do want you to do is to let go of the fear of losing your home just long enough to apply this process in your finances. You could see improvements and "room" in your budget in as soon as one month – just as John did.

Do you remember the "priority spending" example from the Operations chapter? Let's talk about that a little more. In the same way that you should not have paid for that old credit card bill at the beginning of the month, you shouldn't pay for ANY other bills at the beginning of the month. The main priority during the first week of the month should be rent/mortgage. (*Creditors know not to set due dates for the first of the month for this reason. Only the greedy ones who don't care about shifting your focus from rent/mortgage will be sticklers on this.)* If anything else is due during the first week of the month, have the due date moved because <u>it is not a priority at the time.</u> That will free up as much money as possible to pay toward rent/mortgage.

If you don't have enough money after paying your Share, Stash and Save buckets to pay your entire rent/mortgage during the first week of the month, make rent/mortgage your #1 priority in Week 2 – just as John did. Leftover Operations money from Week 1 *(and there should be leftovers because you are not paying any other bills)*, combined with Operations money from Week 2 should be able to cover your rent/mortgage. If it is not, then you may be living outside of your means. Home costs should never exceed 30% of your total income. You may need to downsize to an apartment or home that requires less of your total finances per month. Or, you could increase your income by working part-time until you get it all together.

Fear Of Credit Or Creditors

The Credit Scoring and Information Industry is a billion dollar industry. Millions of people flock to credit score websites daily, subscribing to find out up-to-the-minute details on their credit rating, history, scores, etc. Commercials admonish you to keep up with your score because it could mean the difference between qualifying for a new car or home or getting turned down. You guessed it! That's one more industry that thrives on your fear!

The truth of the matter is, if you can get your finances lined up and begin to live beyond paycheck to paycheck, you will be in a better place to pay cash for whatever you want.

When you are paying cash, no one is concerned with your credit score. Also, once you are living in abundance, you will be in a position to pay off your old debt and clean up your credit. So, your credit score should not be your top priority. You'll have time to fix that later.

Are you afraid of bill collectors? Why? What can they do to you? Bill collectors operate in your fear! A creditor's job is to intimidate you to get you to do something rash. They will drive you to get a paycheck advance just to pay them or run up credit cards just to pay them. Who works hard for your money? *You do!* Then don't let anyone else control it!

In applying the 10-10-20-60 process to your finances, you are moving *away from fear* and *into a faith zone*. You are applying faith that what you share with others will find its way back to you. You are applying faith that things will "right" themselves in your budget as a result of your remaining focused and consistent in prioritizing. You are applying faith that credit scores and creditors cannot do you any harm that you will not be able to undo once your finances are healthier.

Fear of Family and Friends

Listen To The Mustn'ts

Listen to the mustn'ts, child
Listen to the don'ts
Listen to the shouldn'ts
The impossibles, the won'ts
Listen to the never haves
Then listen close to me—

Anything can happen, child,
Anything can be.

-Shel Silverstein

This one's a doozy! I'm sure you can see how this plan could be somewhat controversial among your family and friends. Some of them might tell you that it is not wise to ignore the threats of bill collectors and focus on what you consider to be priorities. Some may tell you it is wrong to deny yourself of some splurges in your budget. They may encourage you to spend in areas that are not priorities. They may want you to loan money to them even after you have determined it is the wrong thing to do. Stand strong! Do not allow others to influence you! Making these changes are the start of changing your whole life. Why would you allow anyone to talk you out of elevating yourself beyond the rut you have been stuck in? Ignore the naysayers and move into your wealth. They'll catch on and become believers once they see the improvements in your life.

The Bottom Line

This system works. I had to wake up one day and admit that the system I was using was broken. I couldn't keep putting myself into a position where I couldn't provide for my family. My credit was so bad that no one would loan me money. I couldn't get credit cards. The only folks who would deal with me were the payday cash advance folks. But they wanted their money back in two weeks and I knew I wouldn't have it for a month - so that didn't work. I was a financial counselor, making good money, but I was making bad decisions – and feeling horrible about it.

Finally, I let go of the fear that had me paralyzed in a rut. I started paying my bills on a weekly basis and organizing my priorities. It was only then that my life made a turn for the better. You don't have to get on the program today. Whenever you decide to try, it will work for you. It doesn't matter how much money you make. It's what you do with what you have that matters. If you manage your money better, you will have more of it. *You can live beyond your paycheck*! What are you waiting for?

Victory belongs to the most persevering.

~Napoleon Bonaparte

9

STICKING TO THE PLAN

Keeping At It Until Its Second Nature

One of the toughest parts about changing habits is maintaining that change. Ask a smoker or a nail biter. They will tell you that even after months and months of applying a new habit, they can still be pressured into slipping back into the old way of doing things.

Every day I hear testimonies about how this program has changed lives. One client called me the other day to say that for the first time in her life, she had money in her Savings account and some in her Stash. One friend who is a teacher said this program helps her get through the summer months of no pay. The testimonies continue to roll in. You can find a list of my favorite ones at the end of this book.

The Not-So-Good Stories

Every now and then I run into someone who has lost sight of the process and fallen back into their old way of doing things. When I ask how they got there, the answer is always the same. They applied the 10-10-20-60 program in their life. Their finances turned around. They started living beyond their paycheck. Then they started spending irresponsibly and ended up right back where they began.

How many of us can say the same thing? Every year, we set New Years resolutions, then start the year off with a bang. We are determined to do *this year* right – whether that means applying new eating habits or spending habits or becoming more organized. We have a plan and we are excited to make it work – at least until about mid-February. By then, most of our New Years Resolutions are as forgotten as last year! Why does that happen? We had all the best intentions, right?

The road to hell is paved with good intentions! ~adapted from Samuel Johnson

Good intentions are not enough! We must put deliberate and consistent action behind those good intentions. Everyday, you must wake up and remind yourself that you are working toward a better life, and that will only come through hard work!

TOOLS TO HELP YOU PERSEVERE

There are a number of things that you can do in your every-day life to help you remain focused enough to stick with the process. Here are just a few that I have heard from clients over the years:

Words kill, words give life; they're either poison or fruit—you choose.

~Proverbs 18:21

Affirmations: Do you know the effects that words can have in your life? I know you don't believe that childhood rhyme that says, *"sticks and stones can break my bones, but words will never hurt me!"* By now, you've learned that words are powerful. You've had enough experiences in life to know that words have the ability to start friendships or end them, to hurt and to heal.

Words also have the ability to encourage or discourage us from moving forward. Do you remember an insult that someone gave you years ago? That's because a negative comment from another person will replay in your mind hundreds of times a day. Positive comments are harder for us to remember for some reason. With that in mind, many people use Affirmations to motivate them through this process. Affirmations are positive statements that are said aloud and repeated. I know someone who posts Affirmations in his bathroom, because that's the one place where he spends time consistently every day! I have heard of posting them on mirrors or dashboards of cars. They should be someplace where you can read and repeat them to yourself often.

Need help getting started with your Affirmations? Here are just a few to get your thoughts flowing:

> *I can and will turn my finances around.*
>
> *I am capable of moving from "not enough" into "more than enough" by being wiser with the resources that I have.*
>
> *I am not afraid!*
>
> *I am courageous and smart and capable!*
>
> *will respect money.*

You can list as many as you want and post them wherever you want! Just read your Affirmations to yourself everyday and watch the difference it makes in your mindset!

Journals: Some people use journals to motivate themselves. Do you remember keeping a diary as a child? Maybe you still have one today. Journals work a lot like diaries in that they are places where you can jot down the happenings of your day or your innermost thoughts. Journals can be used for a number of purposes, though.

I recommend keeping Progress Journals. These differ from regular journals in that they have a unique purpose. The purpose of the Progress Journal is to record your daily progress toward a goal. In the 10-10-20-60 program, you may want to make notes every day about small choices you have made toward spending money differently.

It doesn't require much. Maybe you are proud of yourself for neatly placing change into its proper place. Or maybe you skipped the "junk food" aisle in the grocery store to make healthier and more responsible spending choices for your family. All of those small steps deserve notice! Listing just one item in your Progress Journal every day will motivate you to continue making new small steps every day. It's also very helpful to look back and see your own growth over the weeks and months as you stick with the plan!

I have also heard of Gratitude Journals. They work similarly to Progress Journals in that they provide a place for you to list one item a day that you are thankful for. Over time, this kind of journaling will encourage you to seek out positive things in every day, and change your outlook on life.

Starting a journal is easy. Just find a tablet, note the date at the top of each entry, and write!

Cheering Corner: Everyone deserves his or her own personal fan club. That's what a Cheering Corner is. It's a group of people who will support, encourage and challenge you to keep growing! A Cheering Corner reminds you often that you can finish the job, and encourages you when you don't feel like moving forward.

Your Cheering Corner should consist of people you trust, respect and have access to. The group should not be made up of just your friends or all people of the same age. Mix it up! While it should be a group of people who will support you, it doesn't have to be people who will always agree with you. You must surround yourself with people who will not be afraid to tell you when you are off base, but who also love you and want to see you succeed!

A twist on the Cheering Corner is the **Cheering Circle**. Find others who are trying the 10-10-20-60 program and team up! There is power in numbers! You can meet regularly and discuss your progress or pitfalls. You can learn from each other's mistakes and empathize when things get tough. The camaraderie of a group of people who are *"in it with you"* is sometimes all you need to keep moving forward.

Prayer and Meditation: No matter what your belief system is, you must have some method of remaining centered. Being centered is being aware of yourself and your surroundings and remaining sober-minded about them. You see celebrities on television spiral out of control all the time because they lose a sense of reality. There is no one around them (*or Greatness within them*) reminding them of who they are or what their purpose in life is.

For many people, prayer and meditation are the keys to remaining centered. Both prayer and meditation are ways to quiet your world down and spend time listening to yourself and your God. They remind you to focus on the main priorities of your life and to *not sweat the small stuff.* Making prayer and meditation parts of your daily routine will help you to keep your eyes on the goal of a better, more fulfilling life.

Continuous Learning: One of the best ways to maintain excitement about something is to keep learning about it. The more you work the system, the more you should want to research what else you can do to better your finances. For example, as you see your Priority Account balance increase, you should be trying to read anything you can get your hands on about mutual funds and other smart ways to make lots of interest to grow your new money! Visit the library, talk to people who are managing their money well, surf the Internet for smart and different ways to manage your money better. Make a sport of it! That will help to keep the concept new and fresh and encourage you to continue to apply it.

Keep Your Head In The Game

No matter what, do not become so distracted that you stop the program completely. That will make it much harder to start over. If you see yourself slipping and losing focus, pick up this book again. Read through the testimonies in the back. Try some of these concepts. DO NOT QUIT! You can get the hang of it if only you keep at it until it's second nature. That may happen in weeks. It may takes months or even longer. But you know it will be worth it in the end!

Don't Quit!

When things go wrong, as they sometimes will,
When the road you're trudging seems all uphill,
When the funds are low and the debts are high,
And you want to smile, but you have to sigh,
When care is pressing you down a bit,
Rest, if you must, but do not quit.

Life is queer with its twists and turns,
As every one of us sometimes learns,
And many a failure turns about,
When he might have won had he stuck it out;
Don't give up though the pace seems slow—
You may succeed with another blow.

Often the goal is nearer than,
It seems to a faint and faltering man,
Often the struggler has given up,
When he might have captured the victor's cup,
And he learned too late when the night slipped down,
How close he was to the golden crown.

Success is failure turned inside out—
The silver tint of the clouds of doubt,
And you never can tell how close you are,
It may be near when it seems so far,
So stick to the fight when you're hardest hit—
It's when things seem worst that you must not quit.

- Unknown -

Praise for the 10-10-20-60 Program

"I immediately incorporated this plan into my life and was so excited that I had to share it with everyone I knew. I realize that the key components to making it work are to TRUST and have FAITH that the plan will work and it does. There have been many times that I feared or doubted the plan and my budget suffered that month. I decided that I needed to change my thinking and TRUST that the plan would work and began to feel secure and more aware of my budget. I began to set monthly financial goals and began seeing an increase and loved it! There were months that I detoured from the plan, but I didn't get frazzled, upset, or guilty; I just continued to work the plan. The Plan works, if you simply trust and believe that it will. You will be amazed by your money growing, your bills being paid on time, and simply having a plan you can follow for a lifetime!"

~Tiana Davis

"We are on fixed Social Security income. This program made us more aware about our spending and saving. We were able to save $400.00 in two months."

~Bob and Althea Evans

"It has been extremely beneficial to my everyday living. Being financially disciplined has to be by far the greatest challenge one can face, but I have sought out to be my own "Financial Advisor" with the wisdom the Lord has blessed me with through such a wonderful man as Chad McKendrick. I appreciate Chad sharing this blessing and

I am grateful to God a million times more when I check my savings account. Thanks!!!!!!!"

~Lynesa "Cammie" Sweeting

"We really want to thank you for sharing the program with us. It has been such a blessing in our lives. In the past, we would save money here and there, but when we started the program we were so amazed at the amount of money that we saved in just a SHORT period of time. The program has not only changed our financial situation but it has also changed our LIVES! With 5 children, we definitely needed a financial check up. We are so glad that you blessed us with this program that we have shared it with everyone in our family."

~Derrick and Latrice Stewart

"The 10 10 20 60 program, has given me a new way of looking at and approaching my finances. The program is helping me meet and exceed my financial goals."

~Brandi Hammonds

"The 10-10-20-60 rule has been a Godsend for me, especially being single and a business owner. It has enhanced my knowledge about my personal finances and makes me look at spending in a new light. And most of all, there is still money left after making each allotment."

~La Taasha Byrd

"This system has impacted my life in a great way. It has taken me from living 'check to check' and not knowing where my money was going, to on-time bill paying with a little to save! Before this system was introduced to me I tried to pay all my bills with one check and was left broke on the same payday. Now that I use this system I am able to keep better track of my money, pay my bills on time, and sleep better at night not worrying about what's going to get paid and what did not get paid."

~Monekia A. Wilson

"Wow! This strategy really works! I had no doubt it would. But when you see it by having money in your banking account, savings accounts, a few investments and to have cash at any given time; it's a blessing and a miracle! The amount you make for a living does not matter. This program will work with all income levels. My advice to all is JUST DO IT! Don't be stubborn like I was. I finally prayed and tried it. It worked! It is truly a victory for me and can be for you!"

~Katrina Webster

"The 10 10 20 60 program has been very valuable to us. It showed us a great way to save money and still fulfill our financial obligations. It would have been difficult to begin saving without it."

~Karrie & Brian Pope

"After attending one of Chad's financial seminars. I began thinking of my finances in a more practical and approachable way. I have begun to implement his principles on a daily basis and have passed on the concepts to my daughters, friends and family members. Saving a few dollars each week has not been as difficult as I had anticipated.

~Tyra Owens

Encouraging Quotes

If a task is once begun,
Never leave it 'til it's done.
Be the labor great or small,
Do it well or not at all!

~Anonymous~

You become a champion by fighting one more round.
When things are tough, you fight one more round.

~James Corbett~

Many of life's failures are people who did not realize
how close they were to success when they gave up.

~Thomas Edison~

I've missed more than 9000 shots in my career. I've lost
almost 300 games. 26 times, I've been trusted to take
the game winning shot and missed. I've failed over and
over and over again in my life. And that is why I suc-
ceed.

~Michael Jordan~

About the Author

Winfred Chad McKendrick is originally from Miami, Fl. He obtained his Bachelor of Arts degree from the University of Florida in 1986, and has served as a Financial Counselor since 1989. He sits on several boards, has earned several professional licenses in the Financial Services Industry (including Mortgage Broker, Health Insurance, Life Insurance, and Variable Annuity Licenses) and has several professional affiliations.

Chad has also been actively involved in Youth Ministry since 1986. He received his Ministerial License in 1991, and has served as a Youth Minister, Sunday School Teacher, and Children's Chapel Teacher at Macedonia Missionary Baptist Church in historical Eatonville, Fl for over 15 years. Chad enjoys spending time with his family and being a role model for today's youth.

Chad currently resides in Lake Mary, Fl with his wife Tammy and their two children, Chaddy and Amanda.

CPSIA information can be obtained
at www.ICGtesting.com
Printed in the USA
FSHW011018020620